A Family That Prays presents

Good Morning Lord

50 days of conversations with God to start your day

Copyright © 2025
ISBN #979-8-9927570-6-4

Forward

Craig Jones, Sr. is a God-fearing man whose life testimony reflects the undeniable reality of God's power and grace. Born again as the Scripture declares, he has experienced the transformative work of Jesus Christ, leaving his old self behind to be renewed and made white as snow by the blood of Jesus. His life is a living testament to God's faithfulness and mercy, and it is evident that these words are not merely his own but are truly words from God manifested through this vessel. Readers can trust that the message within these pages is inspired by a man who walks closely with the Lord, demonstrating that with God, all things are possible.

- Marlon Moore, Author of Humble Hearts: A Call to Humility in the Kingdom of God

Check out his book on Amazon.com

https://a.co/d/al8vHus

Acknowledgements

First and foremost, I want to acknowledge my Lord and Savior Jesus Christ for keeping my mind focused on the task at hand. This book would not be possible without prayer and daily quiet time spent with God on matters involving my emotional ups and downs, my trials and tribulations, gaining his grace & mercy for putting Him first. I've learned during this time how to build a real relationship with God and not just focus on being a man who was religious. You see this book really took me out of my comfort zone. "But God!" showed me that trusting in him and putting him first, ALL things are possible. I've been able to witness God's glory, grace and guidance with his word and time well spent with the Master. I also would like to acknowledge my wife Nikole Jones, and my family members who were of great inspiration. The powerful group of men in my Master Life Discipleship class who taught me a lot about having Kingdom values and about not being self-centered and/or selfish. I also want to thank my Bishop, Clifford M. Johnson Jr., and my Church family at my place of worship, Mount Pleasant Church and Ministries in Baltimore, Maryland. Without these people in my life only God knows what and/or where I would be today. I want you to know that every page in this book really involved matters of my heart and how you can use God to get you through life if you remember that he is a real person that you can have a real relationship with, like my Bishop would say, "God has feeling too".

Trust in the Lord with all your heart; do not depend on your own understanding. Proverbs 3:5 NLT

Day 1
Good morning world. "This is the day the Lord has made. We will rejoice and be glad in it." Psalms 118:24 NLT

The greatest gift

The greatest gift is love. God reminds us repeatedly that all he wants is love and for us to love one another. When Jesus was questioned by the Pharisees on what the greatest commandment was "Jesus replied, "*You must love the Lord your God with all your heart, all your soul, and all your mind.'" Matthew 22:37 NLT.*

You can give without loving, but you can't love without giving. "God so loved the world that he gave.... Love means giving up, yielding my preference, comfort, goals, security, money, energy, or time for the benefit of someone else.

"I am the vine; you are the branches. When you're joined with me and I with you, the relation intimate and organic, the harvest is sure to be abundant. Separated, you can't produce a thing. John 15:5-6. MSG.

Jehovah Rapha, thank you for loving me the way that you do and showing me how to love others as you would want me to. I now understand how important it is to love my brothers and sisters, because as a Christian this is what you have asked us to do. I am forever grateful for your love and heartfelt gratitude, providing me with grace and mercy so that I can continue to experience love at the highest level. For without your love where would we be? In your son Jesus name, I pray. AMEN

#SayThat

Day 2
Good morning world. "This is the day the Lord has made. We will rejoice and be glad in it." Psalms 118:24 NLT
No judgment and/or criticism

Many Christian communities are rendered ineffective by an attitude of self-righteous criticism. People become critical of anyone who does not measure up to their ideals of perfection. Some of us may have experienced this kind of destructive criticism. Some of us are also guilty of criticizing others. We need to behave with healthy humility. No one is perfect except God, only he can judge others. We need to focus on our own faults, including our tendencies to criticize others.

You Adulterers! Don't you realize that friendship with the world makes you an enemy of God, I say it again: If you want to be a friend of the world, you make yourself an enemy of God. Do you think the Scriptures have no meaning? They say that God is passionate that the spirit he has placed within us should be faithful to him, and he gives grace generously. As the scriptures say.... *"God opposes the proud but gives grace to the humble." So, humble yourselves before God. Resist the devil and he will flee from you. Come close to God and God will come close to you. James 4:4-8 (NLT)*

El Shaddai, we come before you with humble hearts, seeking your guidance and clarity. Grant us the ability to see your wondrous works around us, that we may rejoice in your creation rather than harboring jealousy in our hearts. Help us to cultivate a peaceful mind, free from judgment and filled with love and understanding for others. Teach us to rest in your grace, releasing our selfish thoughts, and embracing the beauty of what you have made. May we learn to appreciate each other as your unique creation, reflecting your glory in their lives. In Jesus name we pray amen.

#SayThat.

Day 3
Good morning world. "This is the day the Lord has made. We will rejoice and be glad in it." Psalms 118:24 NLT

The Importance of Relationships

Establishing relationships is essential to advancing the gospel and making disciples of all nations. Poor relationships, erect barriers to witnessing.

"Dear children, let's not merely say that we love each other; let us show the truth by our actions. Our actions will show that we belong to the truth, so we will be confident when we stand before God."
1 John 3:18-19 NLT

Fellowship among Christians is at the heart of your Christian experience. Your relationship with God through Christ binds you together with other Christians as the body of Christ. Love for one another is the way we see evidence that we have been delivered from spiritual death to eternal life in Christ.

Dear Heavenly Father, we come before you with grateful hearts, recognizing the importance of relationships in our lives. We thank you for the gift of companionship and the bonds we share with family, friends, and those in our community. Help us to nurture those connections with love, patience, and understanding. May we always strive to reflect your love and our interactions, building each other up and supporting one another through life challenges. Teach us to forgive when we are wronged and to seek reconciliation when there is division. Let our relationships be a testament to your grace and kindness, drawing others closer to you through our example. In Jesus name we pray. Amen!!

#SayThat

Day 4
Good morning world. "This is the day the Lord has made. We will rejoice and be glad in it." Psalms 118:24 NLT

THE POWER OF PRAYER!!

"Are any of you suffering hardships? You should pray. Are any of you happy? You should sing praises."
James 5:13 NLT

Since God has the power to heal us spiritually, emotionally, and physically, prayer is one of the most powerful tools available to us. When we pray to God, we display our faith that he can help us. Prayer is an essential part of the process of surrendering our lives to God. As we share our needs with one another and pray for one another God will display his active presence and power in our lives.

"Confess your sins to each other and pray for each other so that you may be healed. The earnest prayer of a righteous person has great power and produces wonderful results."
James 5:16 NLT

Dear Lord, we come before you are seeking your presence in our lives. You are the source of our strength and hope, and we thank you for your unwavering love. Help us to navigate the challenges we face with courage and faith. May we always turn to you in times of need, trusting in your divine plan. I Jesus name I pray. Amen!!

#SayThat

Day 5
Good morning world. "This is the day the Lord has made. We will rejoice and be glad in it." Psalms 118:24 NLT

Humble, Gentleness and Patience

When we respect each other, we contribute to the unity and peace of our relationships. Disrespect, on the other hand, creates division, misunderstanding, and hurt.

"But those who exalt themselves will be humbled, and those who humble themselves will be exalted." Matthew 23:12 NLT

Unity doesn't mean uniformity—it means valuing diverse perspectives, experiences, and gifts while remaining rooted in love and mutual respect. When we honor each other's differences and try to bear with one another in love, we reflect God's design for community.

"But the Holy Spirit produces this kind of fruit in our lives: love, joy, peace, patience, kindness, goodness, faithfulness, gentleness, and self-control. There is no law against these things!"
Galatians 5:22-23 NLT

Our words are one of the clearest indicators of whether we respect others. Gossip, criticism, and harsh words erode respect, while encouragement, kindness, and truth spoken in love build it up.

"We use our tongue to praise God our Father and then turn around and curse a person who was made in his very image! Out of the same mouth we pour out words of praise one minute and curses the next. My brothers and sisters, this should never be!"
James (Jacob) 3:9-10 TPT

#SayThat

Day 6
Good morning world. "This is the day the Lord has made. We will rejoice and be glad in it." Psalms 118:24 NLT

Protection From the Adversary

When you become a faithful servant of the Lord Jesus Christ. You should always be prepared for the adversary. He is not after the unsaved but the saved. He will use your weakness against you. It could be your Job, friends, even family. His desire is to turn you away from God.

"Stay alert! Watch out for your great enemy, the devil. He prowls around like a roaring lion, looking for someone to devour." 1 Peter 5:8 NLT

Remember that the Sun doesn't shine every day. The rain comes for a reason. We may not enjoy it, but there is a reason for it. Pain works the same, we may not enjoy it, but the experience that comes from pain, teaches us how to endure. It produces knowledge that can be used for your benefit.

"For his anger lasts only a moment, but his favor lasts a lifetime! Weeping may last through the night, but joy comes with the morning." Psalms 30:5 NLT

We already have the victory. Jesus was the ultimate sacrifice for us all. He paid for all sins, not just the ones you committed. ALL SINS!!! We tend to forget the power of God, who is aware of all things in heaven, Earth and under the earth. Pain sometimes cannot be explained but we are never left alone in our times of trouble. God is always with us. Sometimes the experience happens because we forget who/whom is in charge. Man has a desire to fix it himself and that's the sinful nature that can cause tremendous pain by leaning on your own understanding

Day 6 (continued)

"Trust in the Lord with all your heart; do not depend on your own understanding."
Proverbs 3:5 NLT

Just remember God has already won the victory. All we must do is show unwavering faith. Give it to God!!

#SayThat.

Day 7
Good morning world. "This is the day the Lord has made. We will rejoice and be glad in it." Psalms 118:24 NLT

Right and Wrong

Right and wrong as principles are established by divine law. The world today is filled with crime, chaos, marriages that end in divorce, homosexuality and suffering because of God's laws, his standards of right and wrong, are ignored and denied. While man was trusted with a conscious, the conscious itself does not provide a way of what is right and what is wrong unless it is furnished with the information from an authoritative source, which in the world today is the word of God, the Bible.

"Solid food is for those who are mature, who through training have the skill to recognize the difference between right and wrong." Hebrews 5:14 NLT

If man is to continue as a faithful child of God, it is essential that he receives knowledge of evil, as well as good, he must be able to make an intelligent choice between the two. God does not care for blind worship, but loyalty to and trust in him, which is based upon understanding and appreciation.

"They have been a wonderful encouragement to me, as they have been to you. You must show your appreciation to all who serve so well." 1 Corinthians 16:18 NLT

Remember this, it's sometimes hard to do right, but so easy to do wrong. Ensure you make the right choice.

#SayThat

Day 8
Good morning world. "This is the day the Lord has made. We will rejoice and be glad in it." Psalms 118:24 NLT

What are you worrying about? It's going to be alright

Walking with and working for God is a true test of your faith. You see when you make a conscious effort to become a true disciple is when the real test begins. Your new job is to evangelize to men/women and learning to deal with all kinds of adversity. People will disappoint you time and time again. You must understand true forgiveness.

"Then Peter came to him and asked, "Lord, how often should I forgive someone who sins against me? Seven times?" "No, not seven times," Jesus replied, "but seventy times seven!"
Matthew 18:21-22 NLT

Bringing new souls to Christ is one of the biggest challenges you may ever face. You begin to understand disappointments. This also prepares you for handling your relationships with family and friends who can surely bring adversity into your life. As a disciple you learn to numb yourself to world hurt. You understand that your mission is not worldly but a heavenly one. People will be people so why be upset with Gods creation. You speak the truth and if it's not accepted you shake the dust off and keep moving with Love.

"If any household or town refuses to welcome you or listen to your message, shake its dust from your feet as you leave." Matthew 10:14 NLT

You never know what's going on in someone else's life, people come into your life for reasons and seasons. Don't

Day 8 (continued)

stoop to the devil's level when you feel upset and/or hurt.

Use it to grow, process the pain and use it for your good. Just because someone is upset with you doesn't mean you have to be upset with them. We are afforded new grace and mercy every day that God allows you to see another one. Learn to make the best of it and don't sit in your own puddle of upset mess. It's going to be alright; you will survive and depending on how you handle the situation a blessing may be in store.

"Come back to the place of safety, all you prisoners who still have hope! I promise this very day that I will repay two blessings for each of your troubles."
Zechariah 9:12 NLT

Today is a good day, let's smile and be happy. Today is a good day, to smile and don't worry.

#SayThat

Day 9
Good morning world. "This is the day the Lord has made. We will rejoice and be glad in it." Psalms 118:24 NLT

Clear mind for pure thoughts

The devil messes with your mind. He fills it with worry, guilt, resentment, anger, fear, and confusion. He whispers in your ear that you're worthless, helpless, hopeless, and aimless.

"But you should keep a clear mind in every situation. Don't be afraid of suffering for the Lord. Work at telling others the Good News and fully carry out the ministry God has given you."
2 Timothy 4:5 NLT

It's so easy to let the mind drift into places of unhappiness. We can wake up and immediately have negative thoughts. Just stop and think of what just happened when your eyes opened. God has blessed you with another day. Never overlook what's right in front of you.

"So don't worry about tomorrow, for tomorrow will bring its own worries. Today's trouble is enough for today." *Matthew 6:34 NLT*

Refocusing on the good things can bring you joy and a sense of freedom. No need to worry about tomorrow it's not promised.

"And the peace of God, which passeth all understanding, shall keep your hearts and minds through Christ Jesus."
Philippians 4:7 KJV

#SayThat

Day 10

Good morning world. "This is the day the Lord has made. We will rejoice and be glad in it." Psalms 118:24 NLT

Are you working for God or are you on your own mission claiming it's for God?

There is a such thing as Worldly Christians and Spiritual Christians. Which side of the coin do you stand on? You really need to ask yourself that question repeatedly daily. Both have accepted Christ in their lives, difference is one has his own agenda to get things done (so called in the name of the Lord) the other is living out Gods agenda.

"Such boasting is not from the Lord, but I am acting like a fool. And since others boast about their human achievements, I will, too. Are they Hebrews? So am I. Are they Israelites? So am I. Are they descendants of Abraham? So am I. Are they servants of Christ? I know I sound like a madman, but I have served him far more! I have worked harder, been put in prison more often, been whipped times without number, and faced death again and again." 2 Corinthians 11:17-18, 22-23 NLT

People are given roles in church. At first, they are excited, then they become entitled, walking around with the chest out. You know "The I do this for the Lord folks" who are only happy because of the title given to them in church. Don't get me wrong they also know the word, quote scripture, etc. They impress people but not God. Worldly Christians turn people away from God because of their own arrogance and never recognize it. These individuals get upset when asked to perform the assignments given to them. You know. "The THEY DON'T PAY ME FOR THIS Folks" who forget the role they were assigned. They become very important to whom I don't know but suddenly, they're important. It's easy to forget the mission God has set in front of you. Man gets in trouble when power/authority is

Day 10 (continued)

given to them. Folks want to be as important as the man standing in front of the pulpit every Sunday. Not recognizing who is considered the Shepard. The sheep want control. You become so important to yourself that you hurt the church and/or the churches mission.

"Your glorying is not good. Do you not know that a little leaven leavens the whole lump?" I Corinthians 5:6 NKJV

This doesn't just apply to church leaders that have been assigned roles. I'm also referring to people who walk into church every Sunday quoting scripture, singing, shouting, etc. Then they walk out the door, somebody says and/or does something to them and all the church in them is gone until next Sunday. Go figure.... Mad at the minister, mad at the Deacons, and mad at Gods creations (The People). Don't forget we have to do Gods work; his work is hard, and the rewards are great in Heaven not on earth. Your fancy house/car is your earthly reward/payment from God. But not Gods mission. Let's not forget what Gods mission is, helping the church grow and bringing souls to Christ.

"Now may the Lord direct your hearts into the love of God and into the patience of Christ." II Thessalonians 3:5 NKJV

#SayThat.

Day 11

Good morning world. "This is the day the Lord has made. We will rejoice and be glad in it." Psalms 118:24 NLT

It is about the many not the one but the many helps to build the one. The Church!!

"When we bless the cup at the Lord's Table, aren't we sharing in the blood of Christ? And when we break the bread, aren't we sharing in the body of Christ? And though we are many, we all eat from one loaf of bread, showing that we are one body." 1 Corinthians 10:16-17 NLT

It is one cup, but we need the juice of many grapes, it is one loaf, but to make bread we need many grains. The grains must be brought together to make one loaf; it takes many grapes to make one cup of wine. Both the grain or the grapes cannot work alone if they are to become the life-giving spirit; this is what the Apostle Paul meant in his statement that the Lord's people are participants in the one loaf and cup.... There is no other way to Jesus Christ if we don't accept the Lord's invitation to drink of His cup and be broken with Him as members of the one loaf.

For many are called, but few are chosen. Matthew 22:14 KJV

#SayThat.

Day 12
Good morning world. "This is the day the Lord has made. We will rejoice and be glad in it." Psalms 118:24 NLT

Praise Him in Advance

We have a lot to be thankful for, the breath of air that fills your lungs, the blessing of another day, food to eat, and a clear mind, are just a few things that's worth praising in advance.

"Let all that I am praise the Lord; may I never forget the good things he does for me." Psalms 103:2 NLT

Father God, let my mind stay focused on you and your word. Let my cup overflow with your grace and mercy. When the distractions of the day come without clarity, let me not lean on my own understandings and forget my purpose. Continue to keep my thoughts clear so I may continue praising you in advance. In Jesus name I pray. AMEN!!

#SayThat

Day 13

Good morning world. "This is the day the Lord has made. We will rejoice and be glad in it." Psalms 118:24 NLT

It's your season for blessings

The days can seem long and sometimes unrewarding. But there is change coming, change never stops. We have no control over it. The birds begin to sing, the flowers start to bud, spring/summer is on the way. We can't stop change, so why try, it's better to adapt. The only thing that remains the same is Jesus. That's the foundation we should try to build on. The constant reminder that God is with us.

"By standing firm, you will win your souls." Luke 21:19 NLT

Remain focused on the Lord, he is the strong fortress and a provider of all goodness. Become one with the Lord, one mind, one body, one soul. We all can make wise decisions. Why not let your decision be one with the Lord Jesus. There's nobody like him.

"The name of the Lord is a strong fortress; the godly run to him and are safe." Proverbs 18:10 NLT

El Elyon, we accept the changes you give us and are willing participants in your plan. There's nobody like you Lord. We choose to give up our own way and take up our crosses daily to follow you. Keep us covered with grace and mercy. When we lose focus, help us to remember the God we serve is bigger than any problems we may face. Thank you, Father, for loving us and keeping us safe. In Jesus name we pray. Amen

#SayThat.

Day 14
Good morning world. "This is the day the Lord has made. We will rejoice and be glad in it." Psalms 118:24 NLT

Forgiveness when you're at a low point in life

There are so many things in life that can bring you down, a state of depression, attacks from friends and family, work, etc. Sometimes even when you think you're doing a good thing it can cause strife amongst your brethren. Misunderstanding can also play a major role. When your being attacked from all side. Try hard to refocus on the Lord.

"Think about the things of heaven, not the things of earth." Colossians 3:2 NLT

The hardest part when things aren't going your way is to forgive. You are to forgive more than you could imagine. Peter said Lord when people are attacking me and causing problems in my life how many times am I to forgive?

"Then Peter came to him and asked, "Lord, how often should I forgive someone who sins against me? Seven times?" "No, not seven times," Jesus replied, "but seventy times seven!"
Matthew 18:21-22 NLT

Dear Father, Grant me a heart of forgiveness. When things are tough let me lean not on my own selfish understanding. Help me to remain focused on your goodness and mercy. Teach me to understand that this is not the end result. Grant me patience in times of trouble. The patience that you can only provide. Let not my flesh control my thoughts but let the spirit led me to clarity and forgiveness. In the name of Jesus my Lord and Savior, I pray. Amen.

#SayThat.

Day 15
Good morning world. "This is the day the Lord has made. We will rejoice and be glad in it." Psalms 118:24 NLT

As a man thinketh!!

It's easy to let the mind drift into unpure thoughts. Your mind is powerful, it can create a thought and have you upset by just thinking it in a split second. Changing your mind is a powerful tool in your possession also. Just like the unpure/unpleasing thoughts, you have the power to create a great outcome by renewing your minds, when a bad moment occurs think of Jesus, think of all he has done for you over the course of your life. Think of the joy that he provides in dark times and/or circumstances, remembering that he is the light. So, when you're in that dark place, remember that Jesus will always provide a better result if you ask.

"Don't copy the behavior and customs of this world, but let God transform you into a new person by changing the way you think. Then you will learn to know God's will for you, which is good and pleasing and perfect." Romans 12:2 NLT

Jehovah Tsidkenu, thank you for giving me better options to always choose from. When my mind takes me to a dark place, let me remember that I can call on your name in times of trouble and you will renew my mind to pure and please thoughts that will result in a better outcome. You are the strength that I can always depend on. The love that never ends and is always working in my favor. In Jesus name I pray. Amen.

#SayThat

Day 16
Good morning world. "This is the day the Lord has made. We will rejoice and be glad in it." Psalms 118:24 NLT

Unconditional love is what He offers

The love that God provides when you truly know Him is real. Not the I know His name kind of love. I'm referring to I know God because He is my everything type of love. The love that quenches your thirst, love that just brings a smile to your face when you think of him. The love that's been there always and never grows old. Agape love, God is so good.

"When will you stop running? When will you stop panting after other gods? But you say, 'Save your breath. I'm in love with these foreign gods, and I can't stop loving them now!'" Jeremiah 2:25 NLT

"Give thanks to the Lord, for he is good! His faithful love endures forever." Psalms 136:1 NLT

Yahweh, thank you for loving me the way you do. Keep me close to your heart father, for you are my joy in the morning. I meditate on you day and night because of the love you have shown me. I will keep my eyes and head up because with you there is no false hope. Standing with my chest out because of how honored I am that you God truly care for me. Always blessing us daily and providing the chance to love you more. Thank you for giving your life to save someone like me. In Jesus name I pray. Amen!!

#SayThat

Day 17
Good morning world. "This is the day the Lord has made. We will rejoice and be glad in it." Psalms 118:24 NLT

Oh, bless the Lord

"Let all that I am praise the Lord; with my whole heart, I will praise his holy name. Let all that I am praise the Lord; may I never forget the good things he does for me." Psalms 103:1-2 NLT

Qanna, I will always bless your name. Your praise shall continually be in my mouth. You are the light in my darkness. The joy of my soul. There is nobody greater and for that fact I will continue to speak your name from the mountain tops and through the valleys. Jesus is Lord. In Jesus name I pray. Amen.

#SayThat

Day 18

Good morning world. "This is the day the Lord has made. We will rejoice and be glad in it." Psalms 118:24 NLT

The time is now!

O bless the Lord. We desire his goodness. In bad times praise the Lord. On good days praise the Lord. For he has always been good to us. The Lord has taken the heavy burden of sin from us, allowing us the opportunity to be able to do things we love. He has given us the strength and grace to make our lives better and more fulfilling.

"I will praise the Lord at all times. I will constantly speak his praises." Psalms 34:1 NLT

Heavenly Father, thank you for your support and love for our families and friends today as we continue to celebrate Christ Jesus. We love you and we hope that you will continue to support us in our prayers and our hearts. Thank you again for your continued support and love that has been displayed by your sacrifice. Let us continue to hold you in high esteem and honor, for without you we are nothing, but lost sheep scattered across the world searching for hope and happiness. In Jesus Christ name we pray. AMEN!!

#SayThat

Day 19
Good morning world. "This is the day the Lord has made. We will rejoice and be glad in it." Psalms 118:24 NLT

The sunshine's on us all

The day begins with the Lord's blessing. The alarm clock just does a job, the sun is Gods alarm clock for us all. That slight warmth that wakes you is the morning, the light that comes from behind your eyelids belongs to God. Give him praise in the morning. For this is his day. We have plenty to be thankful for, if nothing else another day to get right with the Lord.

"Is like the light of morning at sunrise, like a morning without clouds, like the gleaming of the sun on new grass after rain." 2 Samuel 23:4 NLT

Jehovah Shamma. Thank you for another day. Your blessings continue to shine on us daily. Even on a cloudy day your sun rises. We thank you for your daily presence. In Jesus name we pray AMEN.

#SayThat

Day 20
Good morning world. "This is the day the Lord has made. We will rejoice and be glad in it." Psalms 118:24 NLT

"Unwavering faith" is the kind of belief that stays strong no matter the circumstances. It's the ability to trust in something—whether it's a higher power, a goal, or even oneself—without doubt, even when faced with challenges.

"And now, dear children, remain in fellowship with Christ so that when he returns, you will be full of courage and not shrink back from him in shame." 1 John 2:28 NLT

We are challenged daily by evil. Even a small clip of something can turn you away from God if you're not equipped and or studying.

"Work hard so you can present yourself to God and receive his approval. Be a good worker, one who does not need to be ashamed and who correctly explains the word of truth." 2 Timothy 2:15 NLT

People out here persecuting God for what they saw man doing on a small clip. Notice I said a small clip it wasn't the entire event. And I'm not here to defend no man. But I will always stand up for my Lord and Savior. You see I was on the outside looking in. Questioning everything I heard as opposed to everything I read. Once you have his word in your heart, let no man pull you away from God. The devil is crafty, and his desire is to sift you like wheat. If you don't know, you can easily be persuaded into believing the wrong thing. "A Clip??? Did you know that Judas walked with Jesus and was even considered a disciple. But the power of the devil/money made him turn against God.

"Since they are no longer two but one, let no one split apart what God has joined together.""
Matthew 19:6 NLT

Day 20 (continued)

Remember what I said when I started. UNWAVERING FAITH!!!!

"We who are strong must be considerate of those who are sensitive about things like this. We must not just please ourselves."
Romans 15:1 NLT

I love God. You don't love God? What's wrong with you!!

#SayThat

Day 21

Good morning world. "This is the day the Lord has made. We will rejoice and be glad in it." Psalms 118:24 NLT

Obligations and expectations, things we must deal with on an ongoing basis. Work, relationships, family, etc., can take a toll on a person's physical and psychological health. But we are built in ways that require us to be strong, overcome adversity. It can be a real challenge if you're not in the right frame of mind

"I want to do what is good, but I don't. I don't want to do what is wrong, but I do it anyway. But if I do what I don't want to do, I am not really the one doing wrong; it is sin living in me that does it." Romans 7:19-20 NLT

God never makes a mistake. He will offer you chance after chance to get it right. We must be able to discern the correct path and direction God is leading us in. The older you get the harder it is to make change. If you were a runner from responsibility, your first thought looks for a way out. If you're a strong-minded person, your first reaction is defending yourself/pride. But the Lord Jesus Christ wants submission and to put others before our own selfish ways.

"But Samuel replied, "What is more pleasing to the Lord: your burnt offerings and sacrifices or your obedience to his voice? Listen! Obedience is better than sacrifice, and submission is better than offering the fat of rams." 1 Samuel 15:22 NLT

Let us all no longer run because we all have been called for a higher purpose. We are provided the full armor of God. Just remember this real fact... The Lord said to put on the full armor for protection in war. He also said to just stand no need for you to be aggressive, just stand and wait on the Lord. God is love and all he wants is for us to love one

Day 21 (continued)

another. So, get out of your own way. Remembering adversity is at the door, hard times will come, but we have the power and the ability to call on the Father for his guidance. Learn to pray, learn to be quick to hear, slow to speak, and even slower to anger.

We are of one body and each of us has been given the mind of Christ. NO FEAR

"You will be safe from slander and have no fear when destruction comes." Job 5:21 NLT

#SayThat

Day 22

Good morning world. "This is the day the Lord has made. We will rejoice and be glad in it." Psalms 118:24 NLT

Every day we have dozens of conversations with all kinds of people and face a series of decisions out of every interaction. But how much intention do we put into our responses? Most times, we don't think much about what we say or do, we just act on what we know—which oftentimes can get us into trouble.

He'll drink neither wine nor beer. He'll be filled with the Holy Spirit from the moment he leaves his mother's womb. He will turn many sons and daughters of Israel back to their God. He will herald God's arrival in the style and strength of Elijah, soften the hearts of parents to children and kindle devout understanding among hardened skeptics—he'll get the people ready for God. Luke 1:15b-17 MSG

It's so easy to fall into the patterns and ways of the world around us where selfish ambition, competition, and jealousy are pervasive. God calls us to a gentler way of right living. "Yielding" to others doesn't come naturally—it takes wisdom from above!

Love each other with genuine affection and take delight in honoring each other. Romans 12:10 NLT

#SayThat

Day 23
Good morning world. "This is the day the Lord has made. We will rejoice and be glad in it." Psalms 118:24 NLT

Take my hand!!

When you allow the Lord to lead you, things start to happen in your life that only God can explain. Differences with people end differently. Old friends may leave but God will put new like-minded people in your life to bring forth new friends. The introvert becomes the extrovert. Your communication is different. You pay close attention to what you say and how you say it. You refuse to offend even when offended. Walking with Jesus elevates you to new levels in life. As Christians we are to have unwavering faith in the Lord, and when you allow God full control you even feel better.

"Even there your hand will guide me, and your strength will support me."
Psalms 139:10 NLT

Jesus, continue to take control, continue to lead me on the right path. I understand that the road is narrow, and the path is straight. I choose you to be my guide even in troubled times. I know that you will keep me safe from harm and for that my fear of the world is gone. You provided a new type of faith that I could not have imagined. Strength that I've never felt before. My mind is clear because I'm focused on you and not worldly things. Again, continue to guide me and I will continue to give you full control. In your name I pray. AMEN!!

#SayThat

Day 24
Good morning world. "This is the day the Lord has made. We will rejoice and be glad in it." Psalms 118:24 NLT

There's a time

Ecclesiastes tells us that there is a time for everything and a season for every activity under Heaven. This is why Christians are to walk by faith and not by sight. We have no say in the future. Life is like a puff of smoke everything has a season. There is a time to be glad as well as a time to grieve. God has a purpose for each season.

"Yet God has made everything beautiful for its own time. He has planted eternity in the human heart, but even so, people cannot see the whole scope of God's work from beginning to end."
Ecclesiastes 3:11 NLT

You must remember the Lord said there is a time to sow and a time to reap. The thing to remember is that during this time what did you learn, what's most important and are you helping others? We are only here for a short time. Our real home is heaven the eternal home. So today work on your relationship with God. Not your religion but your relationship with the Father.

"How do you know what your life will be like tomorrow? Your life is like the morning fog—it's here a little while, then it's gone."
James 4:14 NLT

Heavenly Father, thank you for this time. The time to get to know you. The time to praise you, time to worship you. We understand that life is short but the place you are preparing for us is everlasting. Our focus remains in you and our faith continues to grow daily. Give us this day our daily bread for we know that tomorrow isn't promised, and time belongs to

Day 24 (continued)

you. Let's us be thankful for the grace and mercy you bestow on us forever. In Christ Jesus name we pray. AMEN!!

#SayThat

Day 25

Good morning world. "This is the day the Lord has made. We will rejoice and be glad in it." Psalms 118:24 NLT

While you wait….

What do you do when you have a free moment in your day? Are you taking your time to study his word? Are your taking the time to learn what God's purpose is in your life? Don't get so caught up in worldly activities that you forget who allowed you another day, more time and/or another opportunity to give thanks for the little as well as the big things. We can become so focused on our own personal matters that we forget to remember why we even have the opportunity.

"Wait patiently for the Lord. Be brave and courageous. Yes, wait patiently for the Lord." Psalms 27:14 NLT

When you take a breath, when you roll out of bed because your eyes opened another day. Having the opportunity to work, food on the table, clothes on your back, the little things. Thank him for his patience and for his tender mercy. These are just some of the small blessings that are granted to us daily and how we can just overlook them because we think it's just life. No God the Father has blessed you with these things don't take them for granted.

"But if you remain in me and my words remain in you, you may ask for anything you want, and it will be granted!" John 15:7 NLT

Heavenly Father, continue to bless those who seek you constantly. Let the world feel your presence and know that you are God. Don't let us overlook what you have done and continue doing in our lives. I know we can forget but send us gentle reminders that your presence is always near,

Day 25 (continued)

you're always standing beside us. We love you Father, in Jesus' name we pray AMEN!!

#SayThat

Day 26
Good morning world. "This is the day the Lord has made. We will rejoice and be glad in it." Psalms 118:24 NLT

Flowing from my heart

You heard the song before by "Hezekiah Walker & The Love Fellowship Choir." Flowing from my heart, are the issues of my heart…. Is gratefulness. Grateful: grateful; gratefulness. Ask your self today what you're grateful for? There's nothing you can't do without the Lord in your life.

"Let the message about Christ, in all its richness, fill your lives. Teach and counsel each other with all the wisdom he gives. Sing psalms and hymns and spiritual songs to God with thankful hearts." Colossians 3:16 NLT

Heavenly Father, let us not be ungrateful for the things you've already done. You provide the day and the night, the sun and the moon. The food we eat, the air we breathe. Let us all shout with joy about Gods gratefulness. Like the song say's Lord. I could go on and on and on about your works. I'm just so thankful that you wanted to love my sinful self the way you do. Your praise will continually be in my mouth. And songs of joy will flow from my heart. Praise your holy name Jesus. Together we pray. Amen!!

#SayThat

Day 27

Good morning world. "This is the day the Lord has made. We will rejoice and be glad in it." Psalms 118:24 NLT

Delayed obedience is really disobedience

God doesn't owe you an explanation or reason for everything he asks you to do. Understanding can wait, but obedience can't. Instant obedience will teach you more about God than a lifetime of Bible discussion. Funny thing is you will never understand some of Gods commands until you learn to obey them first.

"But Samuel replied, "What is more pleasing to the Lord: your burnt offerings and sacrifices or your obedience to his voice? Listen! Obedience is better than sacrifice, and submission is better than offering the fat of rams." 1 Samuel 15:22 NLT

Learn to listen to God, not yourself. Put your own desires second to what God would have you do in each moment. We are to lean on the Lord for his way of life. He tells us that when we accept him into our lives, he gives us a mind like his.

"Don't copy the behavior and customs of this world, but let God transform you into a new person by changing the way you think. Then you will learn to know God's will for you, which is good and pleasing and perfect." Romans 12:2 NLT

Focus on obedience with God and you will start to understand what your purpose is.

Jehovah-Raah, thank you for your patience with me. I know there are days when the world consumes me. Please forgive my misunderstanding of your purpose for me. I will continue to remain focused on obeying your word. The Bible tells us; *"Dear friends, you always followed my instructions when I*

Day 27 (continued)

was with you. And now that I am away, it is even more important. Work hard to show the results of your salvation, obeying God with deep reverence and fear." Philippians 2:12 NLT. In Christ Jesus name we pray. Amen!!

#SayThat

Day 28
Good morning world. "This is the day the Lord has made. We will rejoice and be glad in it." Psalms 118:24 NLT

God is in control

Just when you thought you had the answer. You should know God gave it to you. When you decided I'm not going to make this mistake anymore, God let that decision happen. When you said to yourself, I'm going to start being nice and or kind to someone who has been a thorn in my side, that was God providing you with a sense of relief. God is always in control. He doesn't force you to do anything, he's just always there in the mist of it all. Always present, always in control.

"You can make many plans, but the Lord's purpose will prevail." Proverbs 19:21 NLT

All things belong to God, let us not forget God creates purpose in our lives and shows us how to live with love in our hearts. He's in control of our lives never forget that. When you make a bad decision and that feeling you get that says. No no no; Who do you think that was? When you have impure thoughts and suddenly something tells you, you might want to rethink that. Who do you think that was? God is always in control, but he never forces you to do anything. That's the pleasure of having Jesus in your life. He always provides a way out of a bad decision. We just need to learn how to pay attention.

"Only I can tell you the future before it even happens. Everything I plan will come to pass, for I do whatever I wish." Isaiah 46:10 NLT

Jehovah Nissi. I'm so glad you're in my life and given me the understanding of who is in control. Let me not lean on my own understanding but open my heart to accepting your

Day 28 (continued)

correction when I'm wrong. I know that leaning on you provides everlasting life and Love. In Christ Jesus name I pray. Amen!!

#SayThat

Day 29

Good morning world. "This is the day the Lord has made. We will rejoice and be glad in it." Psalms 118:24 NLT

It's not over until God say's it over

Put your trust in the Lord Jesus Christ. He is the only one who decides when the time has come. God is still performing miracles for you to see and be witnesses of at this very moment. God tells us why worry, for nothing last forever and we don't know the time or the hour. So, live every moment as if it's your last. Our faith in Jesus Christ tells us it ain't over until God say's it over.

"And I am certain that God, who began the good work within you, will continue his work until it is finally finished on the day when Christ Jesus returns." Philippians 1:6 NLT

While we wait on the Lord, continue to read his word daily. "Work hard so you can present yourself to God and receive his approval. Be a good worker, one who does not need to be ashamed and who correctly explains the word of truth." 2 Timothy 2:15 NLT. Christian's here on earth have an obligation to depopulate hell and populate Heaven. We all have gifts that work for the good of God. Learn the ways which God has given you and use your gift to help bring others to Christ Jesus.

"For the wages of sin is death, but the free gift of God is eternal life through Christ Jesus our Lord." Romans 6:23 NLT

Elohim, let us all understand your way. Let us be good stewards and shepherds with the flocks you give us and let us remain humble with your word and the wisdom you provide us with. Continue to give us the wisdom to know what you wish for us to do and the courage to do it. Don't let our sins hold us back but let us learn to recognize the

Day 29 (continued)

sins in us and use them to encourage others not to make the same mistakes. Teach us to learn how to serve and not to be served. Keep us grounded in your word Father for our hearts only want to serve you and do what's right. In Christ Jesus name we pray. AMEN!!

#SayThat

Day 30

Good morning world. "This is the day the Lord has made. We will rejoice and be glad in it." Psalms 118:24 NLT

Falling in love with Jesus

It's not about religion with Jesus; it's depending solely on the relationship. Learning to love the Lord is wonderful. Over time and continually studying his word we find out how to build a relationship with Christ. You get to know who God is and the love, grace and mercy he has given us. We find out how much the Father loves us and, in our hearts, we only want to please him and show him that same love. Let's not ever forget that Jesus laid down his life as a living sacrifice for us to be connected to the Father.

"Grace, mercy, and peace, which come from God the Father and from Jesus Christ—the Son of the Father—will continue to be with us who live in truth and love." 2 John 1:3.

Falling in love with Jesus is the best thing any of us could do. He reminds of constantly that his love outweighs all. God is the definition of love, and he demonstrates it repeatedly. This also involves his discipline and correction. Someone who care for you does not let you go without correcting any area of your life the needs attention.

Heavenly Father, I pray continually for the love and correction that only you can provide. When I'm right show me that you never stop loving me and when I'm wrong don't let me be afraid of your discipline. I take your correction with honor for it is a privilege to be corrected by you because I can trust that you will always have my best interest at heart. In Christ Jesus name I will continually give thanks, honor and reverence. Amen!!

#SayThat

Day 31
Good morning world. "This is the day the Lord has made. We will rejoice and be glad in it." Psalms 118:24 NLT

Rest in the Lord

Oh, how sweet he is our Lord Jesus the Christ. He provides us with unfounded strength to get through any situation. Our God is a strong tower that we can have full confidence in when times are tough. The grace of God say's just be still and rest, know that I am your God who will always protect his people.

"Be still in the presence of the Lord and wait patiently for him to act. Don't worry about evil people who prosper or fret about their wicked schemes." Psalms 37:7 NLT

God allows us time to rest at home, in the passenger seat, on vacation, etc. He always makes a way for us to rest and now is the time to rest in him. Take the opportunity to sit back and just think about God, rest in meditating, using your thoughts, etc. He has allowed you the time. You would be surprised that when you just take a moment with God how much time he gives back. Never forget the maker, rest in him our Lord Jesus Christ.

"Then Jesus said, "Come to me, all of you who are weary and carry heavy burdens, and I will give you rest." Matthew 11:28 NLT

Jehovah Mekoddishkem, Thank you for the time to just rest with no strings attached. Allowing us time to meditate on you day and night. When we forget to put you first allow us the time to gather our thoughts and refocus them on you. We are grateful for your presence and the opportunity to rest in you. In Jesus Christ name I pray Amen.

#SayThat

Day 32
Good morning world. "This is the day the Lord has made. We will rejoice and be glad in it." Psalms 118:24 NLT

Never be the same

Once you accept Jesus Christ your life will never be the same. It's just impossible if you keep your focus on him. You will never be the same, there's just something that takes over your entire being. He transforms your mind and provides new ideas for you to think about and how to process worldly activities so that you just move different.

"Don't copy the behavior and customs of this world, but let God transform you into a new person by changing the way you think. Then you will learn to know God's will for you, which is good and pleasing and perfect."
Romans 12:2 NLT

Your sinful nature will no longer be in control. It's just impossible to be the same person. Continued study and practice just makes the way you move throughout this earth different. You can always feel God's presence as well as him speaking to you when you're about to make a mistake. It's just something about being one with the Lord that's just so rewarding.

"This means that anyone who belongs to Christ has become a new person. The old life is gone; a new life has begun!" 2 Corinthians 5:17 NLT

Lord God, I will never be the same with you in my life. I just want to thank you for loving me even at my weakest times and/or moments. It's just knowing that with you my life will never be the same. My soul feel's anchored and true stability has taken over of my life. With you Father I know things will be okay even when difficult times come. Knowing that all I

Day 32 (continued)

must do is keep my mind focused on you first and not worldly matters brings me pure joy. Thank you, Father. In Jesus name I pray. Amen.

#SayThat

Day 33
Good morning world. "This is the day the Lord has made. We will rejoice and be glad in it." Psalms 118:24 NLT

Perfect peace

Jesus Christ offers perfect peace, when you accept Jesus in your heart, he offers perfect comfort and happiness. Enjoy yourself while here on earth. We are only here for a short time. Our eternal lives are only a short time away.

"And anyone who believes in God's Son has eternal life. Anyone who doesn't obey the Son will never experience eternal life but remains under God's angry judgment."" John 3:36 NLT

"Here's the lesson: Use your worldly resources to benefit others and make friends. Then, when your possessions are gone, they will welcome you to an eternal home." Luke 16:9 NLT

Heavenly Father. It is to you I pray for my earthly life so that I may spend eternity with you in heaven. I know now that your son is the only reason I have the opportunity to spend eternity with you. I'm grateful and so appreciative of the sacrifice you did for me. Your perfect peace is all I desire and hope for. I will continually send my prayers to you forever because I know that you love me unconditionally. May I never forget what you have done for me. Thank you, Father, in your son Jesus name I pray. Amen

#SayThat

Day 34

Good morning world. "This is the day the Lord has made. We will rejoice and be glad in it." Psalms 118:24 NLT

Everything you need and more

"And this same God who takes care of me will supply all your needs from his glorious riches, which have been given to us in Christ Jesus."
Philippians 4:19 NLT

When you woke up, there was air for your lungs. When you walked into the kitchen, there was food for you. When you decided to leave the house, there was clothes for you to wear. Just the little things we never consider as being associated with God. How soon we can forget that everything was provided by God for us, everything. Never forget even the small stuff.

Jehovah Jireh, we come to you this morning with a reminder that you're the supplier of all our needs and wants. Even when we are in our own selfish mindset, your grace still provides. Let us continue to be thankful for all the things you give us on a daily basis. Let us not forget the small stuff and that you supply everything we need. In Jesus name I pray. Amen.

#SayThat

Day 35
Good morning world. "This is the day the Lord has made. We will rejoice and be glad in it." Psalms 118:24 NLT

Troubled by trouble

When things seem to fall apart, and you feel God is nowhere to be found. Never forget the story of Job who lost it all within a single day; his family; his business; his health; everything he owned and for a very long time God said nothing. Ask yourself, how do you hold on to faith in Jesus when your eyes are filled with tears? When the world closes in on you, tell God exactly how you feel.. let it all out... Everything!!! God can handle it all that includes your emotions. Remember too never rely on your emotions they are like the weather, rapidly changing. God is steadfast and forever unmovable so you can always trust that he's always there.

"Job stood up and tore his robe in grief. Then he shaved his head and fell to the ground to worship. He said, "I came naked from my mother's womb, and I will be naked when I leave. The Lord gave me what I had, and the Lord has taken it away. Praise the name of the Lord!"
Job 1:20-21 NLT

No matter what you feel hold onto his love. Just continue to praise him, and never forget that doubt in your darkest moments, is that same light God provided you with when things were working in your favor. Circumstances cannot change the character of God.

"I have not departed from his commands, but have treasured his words more than daily food." Job 23:12 NLT

Jehovah Shalom, I want to thank you even in my times of trouble. I want to remind myself of your good loving; that you're all powerful; that you notice every detail of my life;

Day 35 (continued)

that you're always in control; that you have a plan for my life and that you will save me no matter what I'm going through. In your son Jesus' name, I pray Amen!

#SayThat

Day 36
Good morning world. "This is the day the Lord has made. We will rejoice and be glad in it." Psalms 118:24 NLT

Putting God First.

Learning to prioritize is one of the biggest hurdles we must overcome when it comes to Christ. As new Christians we are usually focused on the big "I" and or should I say... me first. Continue to study the word of God. Read the entire Bible not just a verse here and there. Remember the Lord teaches us that placing his word in your heart helps you not to sin against him.

"I have hidden your word in my heart, that I might not sin against you." Psalms 119:11 NLT

Don't let yourself settle for the quick answers or remember the same verse. It is a requirement that all Christian's study to show themselves worthy of Gods blessings.

"Work hard so you can present yourself to God and receive his approval. Be a good worker, one who does not need to be ashamed and who correctly explains the word of truth." 2 Timothy 2:15 NLT

Heavenly Father. Thank you again for helping us to stay focused on you and keeping you as our top priority. Studying your word is our life's mission so that we can learn how to walk in your footsteps. Our selfless ways as young believers have us unfocused and only craving milk. As we grow, let the desire for meat become the focus. *"For someone who lives on milk is still an infant and doesn't know how to do what is right." Hebrews 5:13 NLT.* Thank you for your Word. In Jesus name we pray Amen.

#SayThat

Day 37
Good morning world. "This is the day the Lord has made. We will rejoice and be glad in it." Psalms 118:24 NLT

Are you a good friend?

You trivialize religion, turn spiritual conversation into empty gossip. It's your sin that taught you to talk this way. You chose an education in fraud. Your own words have exposed your guilt. It's nothing I said—you've incriminated yourself! Do you think you're the first person to have to deal with these things? Job 15:2-6 MSG. This is what Jobs friend Eliphaz said to him during his troubled time. What a lack of compassion, funny thing is we are all guilty of this same act from time to time. When a friend has a serious problem and has mentioned it to you a few times suddenly, we are fed up. Makes you sit back and think right?

Sometimes we must get out of our own way. Learn how to put your personal feeling aside. A good friend understand that we all make up the one body, many parts, but one body. If a friend is in need and you turn away or shun him/her it's like cutting off the hand, the body will still function, but not the same way. It takes a true friend to endure the pain and suffering from someone else without personalizing it. Some days we must remember that we are all apart of God family and your spiritual family is more important than your physical family because it will last forever. Family on earth is wonderful don't get me wrong, but they are temporary and fragile and sometimes broken by a multitude of things (distance, growing old, and even death). Your spiritual family—that relationship will last forever—will continue throughout eternity. Therefore, we must remember it a much stronger union, a permanent

Day 37 (continued)

bond, stronger than a blood relationship. So don't get frustrated with your friend when they come to you in a crisis, get out of your own way and let them know that you're here for a reason and not just a season.

Seek his will in all you do, and he will show you which path to take. Proverbs 3:6 NLT

Father God, let me be sympathetic when I'm needed for others and not someone who shows no compassion in a critical time for a friend. I understand that when it comes to family especially my spiritual family that I'm not always asked to solve the problem but be there for the person who may be going through a difficult time. Thank you for a clean heart and the ability to understand that with you leading the way, I can readjust my thoughts to be someone who can be counted on when needed as well as a trusted friend. In Jesus name I pray Amen!

#SayThat

Day 38
Good morning world. "This is the day the Lord has made. We will rejoice and be glad in it." Psalms 118:24 NLT

Do You Know Him?

This is not about religion, not about how you pray, not about whether you turn to the east or what you eat, no I'm asking do you know him? I'm not asking do you know his name either remember the devil knows his name. So again, I say, do you know him? I'm referring to the *one who loved the world so much that he gave his only begotten son, that whosoever believeth in him should not perish, but have everlasting life. John 3:16...* HIM!!! GOD!!! Most Christians can quote that passage, but I want to add: *We know what real love is because Jesus gave up his life for us. So we also ought to give up our lives for our brothers and sisters. 1 John 3:16 NLT.*

Purify me from my sins, and I will be clean; wash me, and I will be whiter than snow. Psalms 51:7 NLT. This is what King David said when he killed Uriah and committed adultery with Bathsheba, Uriah's wife. Now if God can forgive someone for that, he can surely do the same for you. Don't be afraid to step out of your seat and accept him in church, don't be afraid when you're having a difficult time in life with worldly matters. Believe in your heart and open your mouth, confess and asked Him (Jesus) to be a part of his everlasting family. God reminds us that he washes away all sins when we accept Jesus as our Lord and savior. See I consider you all my brothers and sisters in Christ Jesus and this message is for everyone. God freely gives salvation to those who believe that Jesus died on the cross for their sins. This is not a gift you earn; heck we probably don't even

Day 38 (continued)

deserve it. But our Father (GOD) does notice all who accepts Jesus as Lord and savior with a sincere heart and grants us an eternal life. Not just life on earth but everlasting life on earth and in heaven.

Pray this prayer: Dear Jesus, you promised that if I believe in you, everything I've done in my past that was not pleasing to you would be forgiven. I confess my sins, and I receive you into my life as my Lord and Savior. You have promised that if I confess my sins and trust you, I will be saved. I do trust when you say salvation comes by grace, through faith, and not by anything I do. Today, I'm turning over every part of me to you.

If you prayed that prayer, join a Church, not a building, a church, one with a good shepherd and begin to learn more about Jesus. Get a clear picture of who your Lord and Savior is and read his word daily so that you can understand more than just the stories in the Bible. Get baptized because this a way to signify a believer's death to the old self and your resurrection to a new life in Christ. It's a public declaration of faith and commitment to follow Jesus.

Now I ask one more time. Do you know him, if not, why not? I love you all and in Christ Jesus name I pray for you all. AMEN!!!

#Say that.

Day 39

Good morning world. "This is the day the Lord has made. We will rejoice and be glad in it." Psalms 118:24 NLT

Lord, teach us to Pray

In belief, our prayers, to be acceptable to God, must express confident faith, loving esteem and reverence to the Father, providing full sympathy with the divine plan and submission to the divine will, displaying a childlike dependence upon God, an acknowledgement of sins and shortcomings and a desire for forgiveness, with humble longing for the divine guidance and protection. This may not always be expressed in words but must at least be the attitude of the soul and/or the person initiating the prayer.

Jesus said to pray like this: *"Our Father in heaven, may your name be kept holy, may your kingdom come soon. May your will be done on earth as it is in heaven. Give us today food we need, and forgive us our sins, as we have forgiven those who sin against us. And don't let us yield to temptation, but rescue us from the evil one". Matthew 6: 9-13 NLT.*

Heavenly Father, teach us how to pray and learn to pray in a correct manner that our prayers can be heard. Thank you for providing us with the Holy Spirit who can judge our hearts in time when we can't find the words to say. We have been taught that *"The Holy Spirit helps us in our weakness. For example, we don't know what God wants us to pray for. But the Holy Spirit prays for us with groaning that cannot be expressed in words. And the Father who knows all hearts knows what the Spirit is saying, for the spirit pleads for us believers in harmony with God's own will. Romans 8:26-27 NLT.* In Jesus name we pray. Amen!!

#SayThat

Day 40
Good morning world. "This is the day the Lord has made. We will rejoice and be glad in it." Psalms 118:24 NLT

Constant and never-ending improvements

The Bible is the only book you can never master and never have enough knowledge of. The Bible is as up to date as tomorrow's news, as my Bishop would say. As a new Christian you are asked to study, study, study, because information will come to you from everywhere and in various forms, some true and some false. We must be equipped with the Gods word to ensure we are being and/or taught correctly. You have some individuals who speak so eloquently, and you may think that person has a tremendous amount of knowledge of the Word because of how they communicate. If you're not a person who takes the time to Study and show yourself approved, you can be dupped by anyone. God reminds us in the bible multiple time of the importance of knowing Gods Word.

"Study this book of instruction continually. Meditate on it day and night so you will be sure to obey everything written in it. Only then will you prosper and succeed in all you do." Joshua 1:8 NLT.

"Study to shew thyself approved unto God, a workman that needeth not to be ashamed, rightly dividing the word of truth." 2 Timothy 3:15 KJV

"For the word of God is quick, and powerful, and sharper than a two-edged sword, piercing even to the dividing asunder of soul and spirit, and of the joints and marrow, and is a discerner of the thoughts and intents of the heart. Hebrews 4:12 KJV

Day 40 (continued)

"Don't fool yourself into thinking that you are a listener when you are anything but, letting the Word go in one ear and out the other. Act on what you hear! Those who hear and don't act are like those who glance in the mirror, walk away, and two minutes later have no idea who they are, what they look like. But whoever catches a glimpse of the revealed counsel of God—the free life!—even out of the corner of his eye, and sticks with it, is no distracted scatterbrain but a man or woman of action. That person will find delight and affirmation in the action. James 1:22-25 MSG

This is what's meant by constant and never-ending improvements.

Heavenly Father, that you for the option to get to know you. Without your word we are only fooling ourselves and demonstrating false faith. Let us continue to be good stewards of your word forever. In Jesus name we pray. Amen!!!

#SayThat

Day 41
Good morning world. "This is the day the Lord has made. We will rejoice and be glad in it." Psalms 118:24 NLT

Never fear Shadows

Shadows initiate fear because the shadow is usually bigger than the source. Shadows are dark, intimidating, scary, but they can do no harm. Definition: (A shadow is a dark area on a surface where light from a light source is blocked by an object.) A person walking down the street depending on the right angle can cast a shadow 10 feet tall.

"Even though I walk through the Valley of the Shadow of Death, I will fear no evil, for you are with me, your rod and your staff, they comfort me." Psalm 23:4 ESV.

David reminds us of that so that our faith will not weaken in times of trouble and/or fear. But I need you to look at it from another perspective. Shadows come because a source of light has been projected on a dark object. You see, you need light to make a shadow. And the Bible describes Jesus as the Light. You need the light to make a shadow, and Jesus tells us he is always present.

God spoke: "Light!" and light appeared. God saw that the light was good and separated light from dark. God named the light "day", he named the dark "night." It was evening, it was morning—Day one. Genesis 1:3 MSG

Jehovah-Raah, your word provides that necessary strength needed in dark times. I now know to keep my focus on the light and not the scary shadows of this world or my past. My mind can play tricks on me that cause unnecessary harm to myself and others. By focusing on the light in my life I can see clearly now, remembering that even in the darkest place a small light can brighten my day. My way of thinking

Day 41 (continued)

about shadows in my past had my mind in bad places, trying to figure out or make sense of what was not even important. But now I have a clear understanding and a renewed mind, continually learning how to focus on your word brings light into my life. In Jesus name I pray. Amen!!

#SayThat

Day 42
Good morning world. "This is the day the Lord has made. We will rejoice and be glad in it." Psalms 118:24 NLT

He is constant

Being constant is challenging. Our minds tend to let us make decisions that can have us all over the place. Trying to figure out the next move can be tricky. Most of us are ineffective because we have never learned how to fight the battle of the mind. The mind is powerful, it will provide a thought and suddenly, the body will run with it, whether right or wrong. There are always things that can cause inconsistency, (1) Your old behaviors and/or patterns, (2) Trust in others, and (3) The devil:

1. The flesh is weak and sometimes we desire to do things that are not consistent with what God has made us to do. It's always that <u>free will</u> that drives us crazy, making us indecisive, scared to move in a certain direction, unable to make a reasonable choice. I believe this is why God tells us to keep your focus on him first.
2. We forget and put hope in people that are also battling with issues of their own. Individuals always want to solve everyone else's problems but their own and that is never a good choice. We have become good a solving other's issues whether right and/or wrong, we always think we have the answers. It's better to get multiple people involved because it provides us with choices and God tells us that where 2 or more a gathered his is also present. We need good friends and associates, a small network of Christian friends who put God first in their lives. We are all of one body when we stay focused on Christ first and our Christian brothers and sisters have

Day 42 (continued)

    real value in our lives when we are all focused on the main goal.
3. The devil is crafty always throwing obstacles in the way, don't forget he has his people on this earth also and some people just don't what to see you doing better than them. They will minimize your situation, make you fill less than, put you down when you need lifting. Be very careful with whom you put your trust in, everyone is not your friend. I know you've heard that on many occasions, and I can say "It's true".

So you must live as God's obedient children. Don't slip back into your old ways of living to satisfy your own desires. You didn't know any better then. But now you must be holy in everything you do, just as God who chose you is holy. For the Scriptures say, "You must be holy because I am holy." 1 Peter 1:14-16 NLT

Jehovah Nissi, I'm so grateful that you are consistent and never wavering like natural man. It's your constant word that keeps me focused on you and meditating day and night on my Lord and Savior Jesus Christ. Preparing my mind for action and exercising self-control. Putting all hope in the gracious salvation that well come to us when Jesus Christ is revealed to the world.

#SayThat

Day 43

Good morning world. "This is the day the Lord has made. We will rejoice and be glad in it." Psalms 118:24 NLT

Mirror to my soul

A primary reason we need courage is the Bible functions as a mirror to our hearts and souls. When we read God's word, we see ourselves, without all the phony ideas that go on in our heads. The mask comes off when you are engaged with God a sight that can be startling at times. It takes courage to face your true self, but to fully embrace the full life God has planned for us we need to take small steps into reality. It takes courage to transform yourself into what God has intended for you. You must learn how to walk without fear when the Bible begins to show you who you really are.

For if you listen to the word and don't obey, it is like glancing at your face in a mirror. You see yourself, walk away, and forget what you look like. But if you look carefully into the perfect law that sets you free, and if you do what it says and don't forget what you heard, then God will bless you for doing it. James 1:23-25 NLT

It takes courage to do what the word says instead of just hearing it. And without courage you will never fully experience the many blessings God graciously has in store for you. Because Gods word is life-changing, we must face the man in the mirror and ensure our souls are moving in the right direction.

All Scripture is inspired by God and is useful to teach us what is true and to make us realize what is wrong in our lives. 2 Timothy 3:16 NLT

Day 43 (continued)

Heavenly Father, I want to think you for allowing me to see myself in the mirror when it comes to your word. For providing me the strength to ensure I have the courage needed when studying your word and finding myself within it pages. Continue to open my eyes to what I see in your word so that I can become the reflection you wish for me to be. In Jesus name I pray. Amen!!

#SayThat

Day 44
Good morning world. "This is the day the Lord has made. We will rejoice and be glad in it." Psalms 118:24 NLT

Sharing your faith

Have you ever tried sharing your faith with people you don't know. They're genuinely receptive am I correct? Now I ask you this question, have you ever tried sharing your faith with your kids, parents, friends, etc.? You know the people who know and/or knew you before you turned your life over to Christ and are usually the people who suddenly can't believe you're a true Christian? Family will treat you like you have a disease. The Bible even tells us that:

Then Jesus told them, "A prophet is honored everywhere except in his own hometown and among his relatives and his own family." Mark 6:4 NLT

It's hard for family to believe you've made a change in your life when you accept Christ. I remind myself occasionally that Jesus didn't come to save the righteous. No, he came to save the sinners. He came to work on the people who needed salvation rather than those who believe they are already righteous. Family will say: don't get holy on me all of a sudden!! Why? I don't know but that's what happens to individuals who fully accept Jesus Christ as their Lord and Savior. It's an overnight change or should I say an immediate change.

Jesus answered them, "Healthy people don't need a doctor—sick people do. I have come to call not those who think they are righteous, but those who know they are sinners and need to repent. Luke: 5:32 NLT

Day 44 (continued)

We must understand that this walk is for you and not to use your walk to impress others. It must be a sincere attitude and real place in your heart accepting Jesus. A lot of people say they believe in Christ; I remind them that so does the devil. It's not your talk; it's your walk, that people usually gravitate to and when your walk is genuine people will notice. God shows up at the right time not your time.

Heavenly Father, first I want to say think you for saving me and helping to build my faith. I take to heart your word: "If any of you want to be my follower, you must give up your own way, take up your cross daily, and follow me." Luke 9:23 NLT. I understand that it's not going to be just an easy road either. The devil is crafty, and he desires to sift us like wheat. Father, please continue too strength me and I will continue to live through your word. In Jesus name I pray Amen!

#SayThat

Day 45
Good morning world. "This is the day the Lord has made. We will rejoice and be glad in it." Psalms 118:24 NLT

Frustration with the word

Are you sometimes frustrated when you read the Bible? This can happen often when you don't understand what your reading, or how to make sense of what you're reading. I hear time and time again that you can read the same verse every day and it will say something different. Well starting out all I got was the same verse every day and nothing different. There are millions of self-help books on how to read the Bible. So, you go and buy one and find out that it did you no good, or you get your hands on a good book that someone usually tells you about and bingo the bright light has become blinding. I attribute that to God speaking to your heart because when you want to know what God is saying he will ensure to put someone or something in your path to open the flood gates. When you are a true believer in Christ, and you want to know something, the Holy Spirit speaks for you and becomes your advocate in communicating to the Lord. Remember God knows your heart, you can't fake it with him and if it is your desire to understanding his word, he will ensure you get what you need at the right time.

"Study this Book of Instruction continually. Meditate on it day and night so you will be sure to obey everything written in it. Only then will you prosper and succeed in all you do. This is my command—be strong and courageous! Do not be afraid or discouraged. For the Lord your God is with you wherever you go." Joshua 1:8-9 NLT

Day 45 (continued)

"And the Holy Spirit helps us in our weakness. For example, we don't know what God wants us to pray for. But the Holy Spirit prays for us with groaning that cannot be expressed in words. And the Father who knows all hearts knows what the Spirit is saying, for the Spirit pleads for us believers in harmony with God's own will." Romans 8-26-27 NLT

Jehovah Rapha, thank you for your patience with me and providing me with the Holy Spirit who can speak for me when I need clarification with your word. Please continue to be patient with me and allow me to grow as someone who doesn't depend on milk but desires meat. The more I stay engulfed in your word the more you open my eyes to an everlasting life. I'm so grateful to be accepted by you and for you accepting me into your family. My desire is only to please you Lord, continue to provide me with the knowledge and understanding I need to become a better disciple of Christ. In Jesus name I pray. AMEN!!!

#SayThat

Day 46
Good morning world. "This is the day the Lord has made. We will rejoice and be glad in it." Psalms 118:24 NLT

Love, pain and emotions

As I've gotten older, I've become sensitive to how I view things, and how I seek out God in this lifelong quest for understanding that involves love, pain and my emotions. My experience has helped me to lean on his word in times of trouble. This has strengthened my love for God and provided a clear understanding from daily study and prayer. There have been times when my faith has been up and down, in those times something pulls at me to seek clear understanding of who God is and what message he is trying to convey. I've questioned a lot, and on most occasions, I've been able to get good and clear answers, some pleasing and others not so much, this usually happens when I don't put him first with my situations. Sometimes I grapple with asking how I strengthen my faith when I can't get my head around "I know I'm going to be hurt again at some point." I ask God how my faith helps correct the misunderstanding I have and why I can't seem to let it go or move on from past trauma or new hurt. The Lord reminds me that you can't change the past, but you can ask God to give you peace with your past and when you do, he provides you with his forgiveness and unfailing love.

Do not remember the rebellious sins of my youth. Remember me in the light of your unfailing love, for you are merciful, O Lord. My problems go from bad to worse. Oh, save me from them all! Feel my pain and see my trouble. Forgive all my sins. Psalm 25:7, 17-18 NLT

Day 46 (continued)

We know that God is a forgiving God. When you accept Jesus in your life your past is forgotten, nothing is held against you moving forward. Jesus was the sacrifice that erased all sins, and I do mean all. There is no wavering with Jesus, and when you are a part of his royal family you can rest assure that your future is bright. The sting of sin/death are no longer in the way, a new feeling of peace comes over you as you continue to walk with God.

Jehovah Mekoddishkem, I'm grateful for the knowledge you provide, thankful for your loving kindness. You strengthen my faith daily as I meditate on your word. You paint a clear picture of forgiveness, and it helps to know that I'm forgiven and loved by you. The pain and emotions I experience no longer hold weight in my life. My rest is different, no more worry, no more pain, just joy. I understand now and although I may cry at night you will provide new joy in the morning. I honor your word and with the strength of the Holy Spirit guiding me my confidence in you has no limits. Thank you, Father in Jesus name I pray. Amen!!

#SayThat

Day 47
Good morning world. "This is the day the Lord has made. We will rejoice and be glad in it." Psalms 118:24 NLT

Balm in Gilead

Have you ever wondered what balm is? Honestly what did you think it meant when it came to Jesus? Growing up I used to hear this song by The Clark Sister, "There is a balm in Gilead" and I would sing it with passion never knowing what it meant. Then I begin to read my Bible and came across it:

Go up into Gilead, and take balm, O virgin, the daughter of Egypt: in vain shalt thou use many medicines for thou shalt not be cured. Jeremiah 46:11 KJV

Babylon is suddenly fallen and destroyed: howl for her; take balm for her pain, if so be she may be healed. Jeremiah 51:8 KJV

I bring this up because I never knew that balm was a medicine used to heal a variety of illnesses in ancient times. It was used for solving chest congestion when used with honey; or lard for bruising, swelling, or damage to skin. Inflammation is what the balm of Gilead is used most for, and today it may be used for sunburn or arthritis. It took me almost 56yrs to put 1 & 2 together when I heard "Jesus is the Balm". You see Jesus would perform many miracles that was associated with healing. Healing the sick, blind, lame, etc., now I can say I understand why the term balm was used with Jesus, the great healer. This just tickled my heart and made me laugh out loud at how we can say things for years and even get accustomed to saying things that we never even know how and/or what they even mean. Just

Day 47 (continued)

going on repeat for no reason at all and how we can repeat things unconsciously without ever knowing what it means or represents. I'm joyful today to know that "There is a Balm in Gilead, and Jesus is the Balm". When you study Gods word, he reveals even the smallest detail to ensure you get the picture, Gods word is amazing when you learn to read it with understanding. That takes time, you see we or should I say most of us can read but do we take the time to know every word we read because we can pronounce it. I know I'm guilty of saying many words without full understanding of what's meant.

So, I challenge you to find a word you have been using almost all your life and didn't have a full understanding of what it meant and do some research, you will be amazed at what God reveals.

Adonai, thank you for all you've have done and continue to do. For opening my eyes and my mind to new things that I have been using for years without understanding. My heart sings with Joy and I dance like King David this morning knowing that there is a balm in Gilead and Jesus is the Balm. In Jesus name I pray Amen!

#SayThat

Day 48
Good morning world. "This is the day the Lord has made. We will rejoice and be glad in it." Psalms 118:24 NLT

Quiet time

There's a time when you're at home and it's just completely quiet. The TV is turned off, no one is walking or talking in the house, the birds haven't even begun chirping yet. It's just completely quiet. Have you ever considered taking that time to spend with the Lord? Quiet time is an essential element when conversing with the Lord. You can spend it reading his word, meditating about God or a good solid prayer session. Most of the time it's usually early in the morning depending on the makeup of your home. Some scholars even call it the last watch, the last three hours period of the night usually around 3:00am – 6:00am. It's just a time for peace; nothing is taking place at this time of morning. Some amazing things happened during this time. It was mentioned in Matthew 14:22-31 that Jesus walks on water to meet his disciples during a storm. When Peter called out and asked "Lord, if it's really you, tell me to come to you, walking on the water." It's also a time when Peter demonstrated little faith by doubting that it was Jesus' walking on the water. Others even suggest that this time holds special spiritual significance, providing anticipation and hope for new beginning and divine breakthroughs; Vigilance and readiness-remaining watchful and prepared for spiritual challenges as well as God's intervention.

But when you pray, go away by yourself, shut the door behind you, and pray to your Father in private. Then your Father, who see everything will reward you. When you pray don't babble on and on as the Gentiles do. They think their

Day 48 (continued)

prayers are answered merely by repeating their words again and again. Matthew 6:6-7 NLT

Use this time as a dedication to prayer, reflection, worship, and intercession. It is considered conducive to seeking God's guidance and aligning yourself with his will. Because of the quietness that surrounds you, you can hear God more clearly while seeking his wisdom and understanding as well as meditating on His word. This is great for becoming a disciple of Christ: *"Then said Jesus to those Jews which believed on him, If ye continue in my word, then are ye my disciples indeed; and ye shall know the truth, and the truth shall make you free." John 8:31-32 KJV*

Jehovah thank you for giving me quiet time. I am honored to meditate on your Word without any distractions. Giving me the opportunity to gain clarity and speak with you during this quiet period of the morning. A time for prayer and reflection and growth within my spiritual walk. I thank you for opening my eyes for new beginnings associated with a new day. Please continue to grant me this time on a continuous basis. In your son Jesus Christ name, I pray. Amen!

#SayThat

Day 49
Good morning world. "This is the day the Lord has made. We will rejoice and be glad in it." Psalms 118:24 NLT

Moving mountains

You know there is a saying in the Bible that all you need is the faith the size if a mustard seed and you can move a mountain.

"You don't have enough faith," Jesus told them. "I tell you the truth, if you had the faith even as small as a mustard seed, you could say to this mountain, 'Move from here to there,' and it was move. Nothing would be impossible." Matthew 17:20 NLT

You see the Lord doesn't ask for much, just a little faith and all will be well. I want to add that sometime a mountain is placed in front of you to strengthen your legs. Hurdles are not always removed in your life, sometimes we must endure a few trials to also strengthen our faith. Things happen in life and when you always walk with the Lord in your mind the devil is working in the background testing your faith. But we have a God who treats us like his children and would never let anything happen to you that you can't make it through to the other side.

As you endure this divine discipline, remember that God is treating you as his own children. Who ever heard of a child who is never disciplined by its father? Hebrews 12:7 NLT

Jehovah Jireh: The Lord is my provider and with him I can endure and move any mountain/obstacle in my way. There is nothing greater than our Lord Jehovah. *Abraham named the place Yahweh-Yireh (which means "the Lord will provide"). To this day, people still use that name as a*

Day 49 (continued)

proverb: "On this mountain of the Lord it will be provided." Genesis 22:14 NLT. Don't mistrust faith, engage in it, we have a powerful God who we represent and because of our love for him, He never waivers. Love the Lord at all times and continue to keep his praise in your mouth. In Jesus name a I pray, Amen!

#SayThat

Day 50
Good morning world. "This is the day the Lord has made. We will rejoice and be glad in it." Psalms 118:24 NLT

Many Names

If you noticed throughout this book I used a variety of the Lords names. This was done for a reason. I want you to get to know him and talk to God using His names. The names of the Lord God hold a specific reference to a multitude of Gods power and his love for us. Get familiar with Yahweh, Elohim, Adonai…. When you talk with God speak to him like a friend or a loved one, not someone you're scared of. You should honor the Lord like we are to do with our parents, are you scared of them? Your parents are known by many names outside of their birth name too (Mom, Momma, Wife, Dad, Pop-Pop). This is how we should love our Lord God and always speak with him freely. Talk to God when you wake up, when you're eating, when you are just sitting around doing nothing, when you're in trouble, when you're hurt, all the time. Get to know him now because soon we will be spending an eternity with him. Now doesn't that sound good, spending time with the Father & the Son. O' how sweet his name is. Jesus forever the same, Jesus unwavering.

Thank you for allowing me to talk with you these past 50 days it has been an honor and a pleasure to let you know how I communicate with the Father at all times of the day and/or night. I hope you will gain a new perspective on how to communicate with the God. And may our Lord God continue to bless you. In Jesus name we pray. AMEN!!!! AMEN!! AMEN!!

Thank you……. #SayThat

Follow us at the A Family That Prays Facebook Page:

And Mount Pleasant Church & Ministries and our Global Connect International Ministry

www.mountpleasant.org

and if you are in the Baltimore Metropolitan Area, come fellowship with us at:

6000 Radecke Avenue

Baltimore, Maryland 21206

Pray for us and we continue to pray for you!

Our goal is to populate Heaven and the Kingdom of God, and to depopulate hell.

If you are unsure of your fate if you died today and you want to be saved, say this prayer.

<u>Prayer of Salvation</u>

Dear Lord Jesus,

I know I am a sinner and need your forgiveness.

I believe that you died for my sins, and that you rose from the dead on the third day.

I want to turn from my sins.

I invite you to come into my heart and my life.

I trust you as Savior and will follow you as my Lord in the fellowship of your church.

Lord, please forgive me for every sin I've committed against you and save me.

I receive the gift of your salvation NOW!

I thank you for my salvation.

Amen.

- Quoted Prayer from Bishop Clifford M. Johnson, Jr. at Mount Pleasant Church and Ministries

www.ingramcontent.com/pod-product-compliance
Lightning Source LLC
Chambersburg PA
CBHW050704160426
43194CB00010B/2001